IMAGINE

THROUGH THE EYES OF...

IMAGINATION STATION

Edited By Allie Jones

First published in Great Britain in 2023 by:

Young Writers
Remus House
Coltsfoot Drive
Peterborough
PE2 9BF
Telephone: 01733 890066
Website: www.youngwriters.co.uk

Book Design by Davina Hopping

Softback ISBN 978-1-80459-308-0

Printed and bound in the UK by BookPrintingUK
Website: www.bookprintinguk.com
YB0528L

FOREWORD

WELCOME READER,

For Young Writers' latest competition Imagine, we asked primary school pupils to look beyond themselves, to think about the lives and inner thoughts of others and to put themselves in their shoes, and then write a poem about it!

Here at Young Writers our aim is to encourage creativity in children and to inspire a love of the written word, so it's great to get such an amazing response, with some absolutely fantastic poems. It's important for children to focus on and celebrate others and this competition allowed them to explore and develop their empathy, taking the time to consider the emotions and experiences of others. Whether that was their favourite celebrity, a fictional character or even their pet hamster, they rose to the challenge magnificently! The result is a collection of thoughtful and moving poems in a variety of poetic styles that also showcase their creativity and writing ability.

I'd like to congratulate all the young poets in this anthology, it's a wonderful achievement and I hope this inspires them to continue with their creative writing.

CONTENTS

The Godolphin Junior Academy, Slough

Thomas's Academy, Fulham

Whitley Chapel CE First School, Steel

THE POEMS

The Life Of A Brown Bear

I wake up under a tall tree
I feel the cold morning breeze
I eat honey from a beehive hungrily
I finish my breakfast all stung up
I go to the bottom of the mountain
I drink the fresh river water
I see a fish tangled in plastic
I decide to free the poor creature and set it free
I see a human and act like I can't
I don't want to harm the human
I see the human trying to spray me
I act in self-defence and he runs away
It starts to rain hard to my discomfort
I find a deep cave with no other creatures
I decide to rest there for the night
I think of my life compared to others
I think I'm in the middle, not perfect but not bad.

Rares Badita (11)
Applegarth Primary School, Northallerton

Stop And Think

S ave the sea as it's ours
A ntarctica, home to 10 to 20 million seals
V ulnerable as the ice melts
E nvironment is being destroyed

T he seal's life is in our hands
H ow much are you aware
E arth is under pollution

S ea is under pressure
E ach seal eats plastic in their fish
A s the sun sets, they slowly hit land
L eft to protect their home.

Olivia Norwood (10)
Applegarth Primary School, Northallerton

Ballerina On A Stage

B eautiful ballerinas dancing around
A lways ballerinas point their toes
L oads of ballerinas leaping around
L ovely floaty dresses
E legant arms moving up and down
R oaring cheers from the crowd
I n the studio we stretch our arms
N ew things to learn every day
A wesome friends dancing with me.

Sophie Tyreman (6)
Applegarth Primary School, Northallerton

Puppy Life

I wake up in the morning
I like to do stretches
Have a drink and wait for walkies
My mum takes me to the park so I can do zoomies
Then she takes me to town for water and munchies
Then we go home for my afternoon nap
After my nap it will soon be walkies again
Back home for tea then it's time for bed
Up in the morning to repeat again.

Amelia Stevens (10)
Applegarth Primary School, Northallerton

James Cook

J ames Cook, I lived in England
A nd I found a planet
M any years ago.
E veryone wanted to know
S o I told them all about it.

C ook was a great explorer
O n my ship we travelled
O nce teachers tell you of my story you'll
K now all about me.

Paige Portrey-Young (6)
Applegarth Primary School, Northallerton

I Am The Gruffalo

As big as a building
As tall as the trees
My heart as grey
As my knobbly knees

Purple spikes
Fearful frights
I've got warts on my nose
You won't like when my jaws close

I like to eat mice
All yummy and nice
Escape don't they try
All these childish lies.

Owen Gazzard (10)
Applegarth Primary School, Northallerton

A Ladybird

L adybird, I hide in the leaves
A pples hanging on the tree
D addy's sitting in the sun
Y ou and me sitting in a tree
B irds tweeting in the sky
I n the tree we look around
R ed and black are the colours of me
D elightfully shining for all to see.

Harry Portrey-Young (9)
Applegarth Primary School, Northallerton

What Am I?

I'm cute like a teddy bear
As black as the night
I'm fast like the wind
With teeth as sharp as knives
When I'm excited I jump like a jack-in-the-box
There's not a ball I can't catch
I eat like a horse
But I'm not as big
What am I?

Ellouise Stamper (10)
Applegarth Primary School, Northallerton

No Mercy

C ombat
C **O** bra
B ite
St **R** ike first
A lways expect the unexpected

K arate
A ttack
I ntimidate.

Luke Boynton (11)
Applegarth Primary School, Northallerton

King Charles III

K ing Charles III is my name
I am the new king of England
N ervous to be the new leader
G oing to try my best to be as good as my mother was.

Tommy Mullaney (10)
Applegarth Primary School, Northallerton

My Hero

A kennings poem

Caring nurse
Rule follower
Loving mother
People helper
Hospital worker
NHS supporter
World inspirer
My best friend
It's my mum!

Eva Ramejkis (11)

Applegarth Primary School, Northallerton

My Dream Horse Milly

A wonderful horse waiting for me
As beautiful as Milly can be
A shimmering white shines so bright
When she jumps up she hits the starlight.

Ellie Mai Peel (10)
Applegarth Primary School, Northallerton

A Lion

L ions play in the sun
I nsects all around me
O n the African Land
N ow it's time to hunt.

Daniel Portrey-Young (7)
Applegarth Primary School, Northallerton

The Drip

I can't fall asleep
There's a drip, drip, dripping noise that's not helping me.
I walk down the stairs, I think the noise is a leak
But then the floorboards start to creak.
I was scared as I ran down the big, big stairs.
But just then I was not scared.
It was just probably the ice melting away
You know the snow melting on the doorframe.
Well I was right
Well I assume.
Oh wait!
Oh no!
It's coming from a room!
As I walked into the kitchen there it was the tap
Well it's 12:00 now
I need to go to bed.
Goodnight from my sleepy head.

Poppy Conley-Mcqueen (9)
Bishop Martin CE Primary School, Woolton

The Life Of The Ocean

I get full of plastic every day,
But soon the people will pay,
The oil from all the machines all full of black oil,
The oil makes the fish die, making them boil,
The plastic assassinates all my fish,
They use them in a big nice dish,
The thunder makes me splash with water,
Making me even shorter,
All the fish swim in the sea,
Going as fast as they can be,
A shark comes hunting for fish,
Giving them a nice, fine dish,
The waves splash right on land,
Covering all the smelly sand,
All the water gets used to drink,
But it goes right down the sink.

Oliver Inglis (9)

Bishop Martin CE Primary School, Woolton

An Astronaut

I am an astronaut floating through space,
Space is an amazing, dreamy place.
I make friends with the planets and play with the stars,
And the most amazing plant is beaming, red Mars.
When it's night, the stars look like fairies in the light,
But if you want to see the world, I have the most amazing sight.
I never feel like I'm falling, the planets are holding me up,
And if you're on Earth, it would feel like you're in a cup.
A rocket flies by so I wave the captain goodbye,
He waves at me back and says, "You can fly."

Martha Benson (7)
Bishop Martin CE Primary School, Woolton

The Sky

The sun blinding my eyes,
And the clouds floating too,
The flowers swaying in the breeze,
And the grass swaying around the trees.
The small, little animals jumping up to me,
One going *cheep, cheep, cheep,*
And another going *cock-a-doodle-doo*!
As the sun began to set,
I turned to a lovely pink,
The animals began to go,
And I couldn't hear *cheep, cheep, cheep!*
Now my time was over,
I had to say goodbye,
I would see the birds and animals
Another time!

Cora Culshaw (7)
Bishop Martin CE Primary School, Woolton

The Lazy Cat

I saw a fat cat,
Stuck in a tree,
It was panting and scratching,
Looking at me.

I tried to help it,
So I took it home,
And I got to learn,
It doesn't like to be combed!

This is my cat now.
Her name is Fluffy.
She is called that because,
She is white and puffy!

She is the best cat ever.
I could never replace her.
She is very cute,
And she likes to purr!

Hope Eos Daniel (9)
Bishop Martin CE Primary School, Woolton

What Am I?

I am a quick creature, faster than a flash
Some call me a climber
Some call me a crawler
I am a predator hunting for my prey
High on the canopy, not scared of anything
I am a beast with black fur
I give a nasty bite with my sharp teeth
You can't jump higher than me because of my great balance
I am average size but petrifying
In a famous film I am a saviour to a small boy called Mowgli
What am I?

Max Lundon (10)
Bishop Martin CE Primary School, Woolton

The Cat With His Hat

I have a hat. A very fun hat,
A stripy red hat, it is a long, long hat.
I am a silly, willy, billy cat.
I hate milk,
Even though some people think it's as good as silk.
It makes me burp like a lion.
I am a cat,
Wearing a hat.
I'm a fuzzy, wuzzy, crazy cat
With a silly, billy hat.
I'm a cat wearing a hat.
Or am I just that?

I am a
Cat!

Georgia Morton (9)
Bishop Martin CE Primary School, Woolton

The Life Of A Tiger

Way, way out into the jungle lies me
I hide in plain sight waiting there maybe all day and night
When my prey has finally come
I pounce out, I don't wait a second
I just eat it all up
I roam around looking for somewhere to sleep
I'm basically a big cat, I'm a tiger you see
Stripes everywhere, claws as sharp as knives
So next time you're in the jungle, beware.

Rebecca Coates (8)
Bishop Martin CE Primary School, Woolton

Winter's Rain

Winter's rain is the best sort of weather
Falling down ever so graceful
All anyone wants to do is play in winter's rain to get you in the festive fever
Little droplets tell you that it's almost over
So you better be ready with blankets and hot chocolate
Farewell it'll be back
And beware because therefore it'll be way worse!

Hope Eyre (10)
Bishop Martin CE Primary School, Woolton

Teacher Chaos

Chatting, screaming, fighting
What could go wrong?
Kids everywhere, pushing, kicking, biting
They all become silent
Like they're meditating
The bell rings
Not for long
They go out to play like wild animals
Run on to the football pitch they all go
Hear the kids from the classroom
Marking books in the staffroom.

Lucie Harper (11)
Bishop Martin CE Primary School, Woolton

The Sky

I'm the stormy sky
I swish back and forth and I glide
When it's noisy you know I'm angry
My thunder goes everywhere across the world
When I'm happy my smile comes out and sparks through the air
When I'm sad my tears go everywhere
When it's dark my lights travel through the world and they shine.

Millie Grant (9)
Bishop Martin CE Primary School, Woolton

My Life As A Cat - For Cat Lovers!

My life as a cat isn't that bad.
I was a fat cat so I sat on a mat
Saw a rat and ate it.
I liked it.
I sat on a tree,
Look at me,
I saw a bee,
I went to a pond,
Magic as a wand,
The fish was going to be my dish,
I was turning also purring.

That's the end my friends!

Laila Khan (10)
Bishop Martin CE Primary School, Woolton

Best Friend

She is kind
When I fall over she helps me when I am hurt.
I am so happy to have a friend like her.
She shares a lot.
She is really funny.
She cheers me up if I am sad.

F unny
R espectful
I mportant
E njoy
N ice
D izzy!

Sofia Duff (8)
Bishop Martin CE Primary School, Woolton

A River

R acing through the valleys
I could feel smooth fish brushing past me
V alleys were as green as paint
E merald grass was bright and wet from the rain
R owed past me dropping plastic bags in me
which sting my skin.

Sebastian Coromina-Adams (7)
Bishop Martin CE Primary School, Woolton

River

Today was a good day,
It was so sunny,
I could see starfish and grass,
I could feel fish crashing into my tummy,
I could hear children shouting,
I could smell food and it was fish and chips,
I felt people crashing into me.

Ella Norton (6)
Bishop Martin CE Primary School, Woolton

I'm In The Sky, But What Am I?

I'm something that helps you sleep
I'm high in the sky
I only see you at night
I live with the stars
I brighten up the sky
I come every day
I disappear at dawn
What am I?

Answer: The moon.

Prasannya Nadarajah (9)
Bishop Martin CE Primary School, Woolton

Down Into The Basement

Down into the basement of the haunted house.
I am as scary as a ghost.
I am as big as a vampire.
I am sharper with my eyes than my teeth.
I want to live in the attic with all of the spiders.

Cameron Pilkington (8)
Bishop Martin CE Primary School, Woolton

A River

Today I am feeling happy
I can taste sea salt I try to spit it out
I can hear seagulls squawking, I try to stop them
I can feel fish tickling my feet although they can't help it.

Robyn Da Costa Greaves (6)
Bishop Martin CE Primary School, Woolton

Summer

S ummer is here
U nderwater in the pool
M ummy gives me ice cream
M y family go outside
E very day is hot
R ed cheeks in the sun.

Evangeline Chidwick (5)
Bishop Martin CE Primary School, Woolton

A River

R ain going down my body,
I want it to stop,
V ibrant flowers so beautiful,
E very single day it's the same,
R ain stopped now.

Prathiga Nadarajah (6)
Bishop Martin CE Primary School, Woolton

Winter

W inter is very cold
I nside it is warm
N ights get longer
T ime to get warm
E ach tree has no leaves
R eally deep snow.

Connor Pilkington (5)
Bishop Martin CE Primary School, Woolton

River

I am feeling blue today
Thunder was crashing
Clouds were grey
Plastic bags sting my body
People are splashing in me
And I will sail with my body.

Isaac Losh (6)
Bishop Martin CE Primary School, Woolton

T-Rex

A kennings poem

Meat eater
Giant stomper
Slow mover
Child scarer
Teeth barer
Eye widener
Master roarer
Ground shaker
Blood sucker.

Vincent Young (7)
Bishop Martin CE Primary School, Woolton

We Are Friends Forever And Ever

M y lovely best, best friends
Y ou and me forever friends

B ecause no one knows me better than you
E xpect when you make me feel upset
S o this makes you
T he worst friend in the world

F riends are the best all time
R evenge is not the best all time
I think that I always need a friend
E ver and ever best friend
N eed to go and play together
D on, you can be my friend.
S un watching us together.

Amber Sargent (8)
Elm Road Primary School, Wisbech

Pretty Butterfly

One day a butterfly was flying around me,
It landed on my nose and I sneezed.
It flew away from me
And then the butterfly landed on my arm.
Then I ran and the butterfly stayed with me.
The butterfly is so cute.
I slept with it and we had a good night's sleep
And then the next day it was Halloween.
We had lots of fun eating sweets
And it was so good to eat with my friend.
We had a little adventure because he is my best friend.
We lived happily ever after.

Alana McCourt (8)
Elm Road Primary School, Wisbech

Black And Mysterious

I'm black and beautiful
You can fall in love with me in one look
I'm as loud as a rock concert
I can be loving
I can be mean
I can fight
I'm mostly lonely
I can climb like a master but sometimes I can't get down
I'm the Queen of Cuteness
What am I?

Answer: I'm a black cat.

Liva Hartmane (9)
Elm Road Primary School, Wisbech

Cute And Fluffy

Cute and fluffy,
Worthy purchase,
Small and furry,
Vegetarian appetite,
Nice and pretty,
Not always hungry,
I am imaginative,
Creative, white like snow,
Not even a carnivore,
Frightened by the leopard's roar.
What am I?

Answer: A rabbit.

Shea Augustin (9)
Elm Road Primary School, Wisbech

Great Strength

I am strong
But I have skinny legs.
I have big eyes.
I am small.
I have a big appetite.
I have six legs
And I run really fast.
I have to work for our queen.
I'm an insect.
What am I?

Answer: An ant.

Daniils Hrebtovs
Elm Road Primary School, Wisbech

What Am I?

Soft as a fluffy pillow.
Cute as a little cat.
Fluffy as a baby bear.
Little as a cute mouse.
Playful as a little kid.
Fast as a bike.
Kind as an angel.
Explores like a little explorer.
Loves people.
What am I?

Emilia Tlock (9)
Elm Road Primary School, Wisbech

Apples Fall From My Fingers

W ood everywhere
O ld trees still alive
O ld and still look good
D amp and foggy
L ight shine through my leaves
A pples fall from my fingers
N ice and calm
D amp and nice.

Archie Robinson (8)

Elm Road Primary School, Wisbech

A Jungle Friend

A kennings poem

Fruit eater
Tree knocker
Big tusks
Long trunk
Whooshing tail
Big thud
Walking slow
Here we go
Eating leaves
Sleeping peacefully
What am I?

Answer: I am an elephant.

Lily Carter (9)
Elm Road Primary School, Wisbech

The Outside

Oxygen cleaner
Green and greener
Brown bar
Twenty branches
Apples, pears
Falling leaves
Falling bark
Brown and black
Dirty roots.
What am I?

Answer: A tree.

Aronas Bernatonis (8)
Elm Road Primary School, Wisbech

Who Am I?

A kennings poem

Homework eater
Outdoor lover
Ball lover
Foot eater
Slipper wrecker
Mud roller
Water liker
Sea lover
Treat stealer
Who am I?

Answer: A husky puppy.

Lawson Humphreys (8)
Elm Road Primary School, Wisbech

Big And Red

I am as slithery as a snake.
I can fly.
My skin is strong.
I look scary.
I'm red and I breathe fire.
I'm as big as a house.
What am I?

Answer: A dragon.

Yaqoob Anjum (8)
Elm Road Primary School, Wisbech

What Am I?

A kennings poem

Rabbit eater
Mountain liver
Night hunter
Brave defender
Pretty pattern
Skinny animal
Cute eyes
Black whiskers
Soft fur
King of lightning.
I am a leopard.

Aironas Ruibys (9)
Elm Road Primary School, Wisbech

The Riddle

I am as big as a house.
My wings are like a devil's.
Horns like a point.
I have a tail, it's very long.
I breathe fire.
What am I?

Answer: A dragon.

Kymii Gowler (8)
Elm Road Primary School, Wisbech

Tiny Walker

A kennings poem

Sharp teeth
Small sprinter
Little legs
Rough scales
Small scarer
Long tail
Sonic legs
Whispering hiss.
What am I?

Answer: A lizard.

Vanesa Vasko (8)
Elm Road Primary School, Wisbech

What Am I?

A kennings poem

Cat runner
Stone eater
A sleeper
Beautiful coat
Cute face
Ear mover
Awesome licker
What am I?

Answer: A British short hair.

Edward Slamas (8)
Elm Road Primary School, Wisbech

Trash Eater

A kennings poem

Trash eater,
Sparkly clawer,
Scratchy clawer,
Rabbit eater,
Bird snatcher,
Biting teeth,
Hunting thief,
Wet tongue,
I am a fox.

Lucian Boughen (8)
Elm Road Primary School, Wisbech

Big Red Monster

I'm as big as a girl.
I'm as moody as a told-off child.
I'm as red as fire.
What am I?

Answer: Anger.

Riley Montgomery (8)
Elm Road Primary School, Wisbech

The White Cuddly Kitten

I was playing outside
When I saw a white cat
Appearing in my garden.
I didn't know what to do
So I ran inside my home.

Paula Prancane (9)
Elm Road Primary School, Wisbech

Dogs Rule

People lover
Food hunter
Tummy rubs
Is very effective for him to love you forever.
Woof!
I'm a dog.

Brayden Gant (8)
Elm Road Primary School, Wisbech

Ginger Cat

I know a ginger cat,
Walking by the school,
It's really so fat,
And it looks so cool,
We all love it,
She knows that and uses us all,
It never annoys us, I think it knows the rules,
Maybe a rat would be a good boon,
My beautiful ginger cat, I really adore you,
Don't go far,
We can't go home without seeing you.

Zainah Alokkah (9)
Falconbrook Primary School, Battersea

My Little Dream

My little dream...
You'll be with me!
We will never fall apart!

My sweet dream...
Stay with me!
Forever never leave me!
It is going to be just me and you against the world!

My sweetest dream on Planet Earth,
Stay with me!
My little dream...

Adelina Nikolova (8)
Falconbrook Primary School, Battersea

Car

I love cars, I love cars,
You can go anywhere with cars,
Cars can protect from rain,
I love cars, I love cars,
Cars can travel safely,
Cars can lift heavy things,
Cars are so relaxing,
Cars can go anywhere.

Shahzad Shabir (8)
Falconbrook Primary School, Battersea

Friends

F abulous
R eady, set, go
I ncredible
E very day we're kind
N ice and kind
D one!
S uper-duper.

Alana Stewart
Falconbrook Primary School, Battersea

The Rescued Cat

I am walking in the gloomy park.
It is super dark.
I am happy in the gloomy park.
It is quiet like a butterfly that never talks.
I am now sad in the gloomy park.
I don't have an owner.
I have nobody to talk to.
I can hear the blowing wind.
My furry tail is waving
Back and forth.
I can see the grass soaking with saltwater rain.
I can feel the wet grass on my black and brown paws.
I can hear the thunder coming near my black ears.
I can smell the dirty mud in the park.
I am walking in the park and the sun is rising up.
There's a girl walking towards me.
I am shivering as she picks me up.
I feel warm in her arms.
It's not gloomy anymore.
I feel happy.

I feel joyful.
I am a black and brown cat with my owner.

Simran Kaur (9)
Ibrox Primary School, Ibrox

Moonlight In The Box

I am trapped in a box.
I have Teddy with me.
Teddy is my favourite.
I smell my food.
It smells as good as chicken.
I hear cars going fast and people chatting.
I can see a girl picking up my box.
My ears are black and sticking out of the box.
I am feeling good about this.
My body is feeling excited.
Maybe the girl is taking me to an animal shelter.
Maybe she's taking me to her palace.
Maybe she's rich.
We are at her white palace.
I am a lucky cat.

Aleeza Beg
Ibrox Primary School, Ibrox

A Wild Pony

Walk, trot, canter,
Gallop, gallop through the trees, through the forest, through the leaves,
Burrs in my mane and tail, rushing, rushing,
Wind bashing and thrashing,
The sun hitting my face,
Feeling weak, weak and tired,
Gallop, canter on through the forest, through the trees,
To a field of fallen leaves,
I go and rest under a tree,

I wake, I see before me,
A herd of wild moor ponies,
I join their gallop, canter, run,
On and on we go into the distance on and on!

Harriet Falconer (9)
Lawford CE Primary School, Lawford

The Life Of A Pichu

I am a Pichu, I have no family, I am alone,
Then Cubone comes up with his big bone,
My home is in a hollow of a tree,
I'd like to find a friend as soon as can be.

Now it is night,
And I don't want to get into a fright,
Now it is bed,
And time to rest my head.

It is morning and it is sunny,
I like zapping trainers, I find it funny,
I try to get food from the berry bush but I always get trampled and stamped by Pokémon trying to get food,
Now I am not in a good mood.

Whenever Eternatus comes, I hide in my hole,
And eat fruit from my fruit bowl,
I can cut branches off trees with my tail,
I try to get a berry from a tree but Pidgey takes it, making me fail.

I have made a friend,
Steene, Steene likes to send,
Letters to my door,
Tonight I can't sleep because Abra likes to snore.

Toby George (9)

Lawford CE Primary School, Lawford

Laptop Loneliness

A laptop freshly made,
Just came out of the window
But people are only using the old laptops they bought.

Sitting here for decades not a pound's worth in me.

Every day I see people walking,
Day after day, week after week, month after month, year after year.

Even though they buy other laptops,
I am the oldest in the shop,
No one will buy me,
People walk by and laugh at me.

I think every day is going to be an endless loop.

But one day,
I thought someone had bought me.

But they threw me away.

I was really happy when they picked me up,
But they threw me away,
I fell and the dark days came.

I'm flying away and it feels like everyone walked past me,
In an endless abyss,
Why will they not buy me?
I'm really lonely.

Jacob Jones (9)
Lawford CE Primary School, Lawford

A Day In The Life Of A Guinea Pig

I can see Twirl,
She is greedy, crazy and fluffy,
Me on the other hand,
I am Topsy,
I am greedy, clever and have silky fur.

I can see our food bowl,
Full of yummy, crunchy and dark maroon food.

I can smell the hay,
Sweet, natural, syrupy hay.

I can smell the grass,
Damp, fragrant and fresh grass.

I can hear the birds,
Happy, singing, whistling birds.

I can hear Magnum and Batman
Purring, shrieking and squealing.

I can taste the carrots,
Lovely, crunchy, sugary carrots.

I can taste the cardboard,
Durable, chewy, stiff cardboard.

I can feel the sawdust,
Dry, soft, squishy sawdust.

I can feel the straw,
Cosy, warm, bristly straw.

Barnaby Whitworth (10)

Lawford CE Primary School, Lawford

The Life Of A Treecko

I am a Treecko owned by Professor Rowan
About to be given away
My trainer's name is Barry
I like to call him sensei.

I am now evolving
And I have won
I am now a Groyvle
So this battle is done.

I have made some friends
Breloom, Shiftry and Walrein
And when I have free time
You will see me train.

Now I evolve again
I am turning white
I am now a Sceptile
My opponents are in fright.

Off to Kalos I go
A search for a mega stone

And with the Hoenn League
I sit on the throne.

With Hoenn I'm done
Where to go
I can't choose
Alola, Galar or Sinnoh.

Ben Neethling (9)

Lawford CE Primary School, Lawford

Astronauts In Space

S pacemen live in a black space,
P eople at the age of sixteen can start training till eighteen,
A s an astronaut has to do tasks,
C ats will go to space and I will bring them,
E gg lovers, just to say you can't make eggs in space.
M en in space get lazy bones from no gravity,
A nti-gravity is bad for your body because you can accidentally spin,
N eon space suits aren't allowed in space because it might distract the space captain.

Andre (9)
Lawford CE Primary School, Lawford

Fruit Bowl

F unny-looking fruit bowl,
R ests on the oven,
U nder me a grape named Tom has shrivelled up,
I 'm the only thing left sometimes...
T o the day I was bought I was happy.

B ut now it's not it's sad being lonely,
O ut of fruit, never refilled,
W hile the people walk past me my spots come off,
L uscious juicy pineapple, yummy scrumptious apples, they're never there...

Florence Jones (10)
Lawford CE Primary School, Lawford

The Devil Teacher

Have you ever wondered
What a teacher does at night?
Maybe they just mark and check work,
Maybe they just stay at school.
Just being useless.

But... What if...?

They lurk in your bedroom,
Stealing information,
What's that?
You're home alone on Sunday?
So, if you happen to stumble into a teacher at night,

Run for your life!

Ella (9)
Lawford CE Primary School, Lawford

The Worrying War

Noise all around me,
Bombs exploding everywhere,
This is a nightmare,
I'm on a train,
Soldiers are in pain,
My gas mask around my neck.
Bag on my back,
Air raid sirens are whirring,
I'm waving goodbye to
My mum's murmuring,
Planes in the air, dark on the street,
Soldiers are fighting.

Poppy Jordan (9)
Lawford CE Primary School, Lawford

What Am I?

Tall, long, I stalk through the night,
Killing and hunting is my right.
Living in winter north of Russia,
I am silent and fast creeping up behind.
I leap for prey then bite. Killing, killing, dead.
A deadly, killing, stalking, hunting, machine.
What am I?

Answer: A Siberian Tiger.

Jamie Smith (9)
Lawford CE Primary School, Lawford

My Dog Merlot

My dog is a trickster.
She would love to lick ya.
If she smells treats
Make sure she gets to eat.

She loves walks.
Sometimes she even talks.
When she barks
She sounds like a shark.

Sometimes I am bad.
That makes me sad.
I love my family
I will live happily.

Ophelia Deane (10)
Lawford CE Primary School, Lawford

Leo The Cat

L oves cat pouches
E ats chicken and roast beef
O ff, I'm under the sofa

T homas is round
H ow do I escape?
E at, eat, eat

C rash, crash, crash
A rgh, the children are killing me
T his is the time.

Christian Vaughan (9)
Lawford CE Primary School, Lawford

My Cat

A kennings poem

Mouse chaser
Tuna eater
Milk lover
Chocolate hater
Treat eater
Tree climber
Orange hater
Big hunter
Silent killer
Giant eater
Catnip lover
Lazy sleeper
Rat killer
Movie watcher
Human lover
Paw licker.

Chris (9)
Lawford CE Primary School, Lawford

Worry Monster

I'm the Worry Monster always listening
I'm always watching
Always taking notes
When you're worried you put a worry in me
And I keep it safe
I'm soft and cool
I have big eyes
I'm funny
I put a smile on your face.

Lola Hislop (9)
Lawford CE Primary School, Lawford

Pebbles The Guinea Pig

P retty and very cute
E ating all day every day
B ig appetite
B lack, beige and white is her colour
L apping up her food every day
E nding her day with a nibble
S ending herself running all the time.

Elliot Robinson (9)
Lawford CE Primary School, Lawford

What Am I?

I am always there for the match.
My position is everywhere even in goal,
I can fly really high in the air.
I am really fast.
I get lots of goals for my team.
What am I?

Answer: A football.

Thomas Leeke (9)
Lawford CE Primary School, Lawford

What Am I?

I get kicked every day and night,
I'm a sphere,
I can be any colour,
After a match I feel so invisible,
And I have so many bruises.
What am I?

Answer: A football.

Milana Zelionyte (10)
Lawford CE Primary School, Lawford

What Am I?

I get walked daily
I like to play with my toys
I don't really like the car
I get fed morning and night
I'm not allowed in the park.
What am I?

Answer: A dog.

Oscar Worden (9)
Lawford CE Primary School, Lawford

Dog Life

I can smell all the smells in the air,
I can smell everything, even the food over there,
I am on my way for a walk,
But my owner keeps on stopping to talk,
With people with their own pets,
But I can tell they just want to get to the vet,
Finally, we get to the park,
And we see one of the city's landmarks,
And my owner takes out my tennis ball,
Then gives it a ginormous haul,
I go retrieve it, I can achieve it,
My owner's very happy, and I'm her favourite chappy!

Evie Ayres (9)
Meon Junior School, Southsea

Our Queen

Her Majesty was great
She had such a caring mind
Fair and so very kind
We'll never forget our Queen

Her Majesty was wise
She loved horse rides
Walking corgis underneath glorious skies
Our truly awesome Queen

Jubilees aplenty
Silver, golden to name a few
She was lucky enough to reach a diamond and platinum too
She was our inspiration, our Queen

She kept her promise to us all
She will forever be known as the best queen
We'll love her forever
Our special Queen

Sadly now she's gone to rest
She really, truly did the best

Now we have the queen's eldest son
To ensure the queen's legacy lives on
Long live the longest-reigning Queen!

Amelia Dutton (10)
Meon Junior School, Southsea

Trick Or Treating Tonight

Putting on my costume,
Ready for tonight.
Knocking on doors,
And giving people a fright.
People giving away candy,
Taking one or two,
Hunting down every house,
Going to shout boo!
Scary bats and bones,
Banging on your door.
Pressing the bell with spooky sounds,
Being scared even more.
Filling up my bucket,
All the way to the top.
Trick or treating had ended,
It's time to stop!

Ellie Day (10)
Meon Junior School, Southsea

The Imaginary Monster

I woke up in the morning with birds going *tweet, tweet*.
When I got out of bed *creep, creep, creep,*
I tiptoed over to my sister's phone,
But then she had a groan.
I was going downstairs,
But I saw green bulging eyes,
Two pointy horns.
So then I screamed, "*Arghh!*"
Then the monster said, "Wait."
I went down again and turned on the lights,
There were two blue glues that looked like horns,
And two green fans that looked like bulging eyes,
But then I think again that it was true.

Heidi Barnard (8)
St Edmund's Preparatory School, Old Hall Green

The Pain Of Ukraine

The war in Ukraine simply has no gain,
It's only part of Putin's game,
To destroy the grain's chain,
Planes, trains and spreading the wrong campaign.

It's insane that the gas main,
Is not being maintained,
As Russia continues to blame
And look down with disdain on Ukraine.

It's becoming a bloodstain to obtain
More domain and increasing its reign
On many of the territories of Ukraine,
Where people have been slain in vain.

Lorenzo Hookham (10)
St Edmund's Preparatory School, Old Hall Green

Freedom

As I gallop
Through meadows and fields,
The rest of the herd guard me like shields.
I am safe yet so free,
So neighbourly yet so independent

I feel wind in my mane,
And sun on my back,
Then we stop by a lake to have a quick snack.
I am content yet so free,
So respected yet so disciplined

My name is Midnight,
I am a horse,
And this is *freedom!*

Jessica Northen (10)
St Edmund's Preparatory School, Old Hall Green

Windy Willow

In the dark creeps of the forest
Is the willow tree
The tree is like a twist of lime on your tongue
With rutted roots lying down in the grass
And a red ruby dot of a mushroom nestled in
the roots.
In the distance
In the crisp, cold north, is a great old oak.
The great, old oak is home to all types of animals
Like a big mother.

Emily Welberry (10)
St Edmund's Preparatory School, Old Hall Green

Tula In The Garden

My name is Tula
I love to sniff in the garden
And I'm particularly fond
Of chasing squirrels and rabbits
Which is one of my particularly bad habits
Then I go and have a quick nap in the sun
And that is the day and the life of Tula done.

Ellie Northen (8)
St Edmund's Preparatory School, Old Hall Green

Cupcake

I'm small and round and very sweet
People say I'm such a treat
I'm often found with lots of friends
Come out mostly on weekends
I'm soft and fluffy, airy and light
But then somebody takes a...

Ariana Curran (8)
St Edmund's Preparatory School, Old Hall Green

Oscar

O scar is my fluffy cat
S itting in the house all day he
C leans himself
A fter he has eaten his meaty dinner
R uns around the house.

Alexander Ivnik-Sotiriou (8)
St Edmund's Preparatory School, Old Hall Green

House To House

I am a house as tall as I can be,
I can be like a skyscraper or small like a cottage.
Big like a mansion or warm like a bunker.
I can be on top of a restaurant, a shop or in a truck
I can be cold like an igloo or hot like a sauna.
Quiet like a library or loud like a rock house.
I can be located in rich countries, poor countries, war countries, safe countries. I am everywhere, from England to Jamaica to China to Mexico I can be found.
I can be found in odd places like underwater or in space.
Wherever you go I am there.

Zachary Deveny (10)
St Edward's CE (VA) Primary School, Romford

Owl

I am just an owl,
In my name I only have one vowel,
And I really hope no one sees
Me having a talk with the trees,
Because then they will think, "How?"

I love my family,
Mother, brother and me,
And if you ask of my father,
I think I would rather
Jump on a needle and say, "Aeee!"

I know how to write with a pen.
(Shh... this paper was sat on by a hen)
You should give me a pat,
But I'm not a big, furry cat,
(And I can't pronounce 'n').

Matthew Koczorowski (8)
St Edward's CE (VA) Primary School, Romford

Owl

I am an owl,
In the trees,
I float up high,
Through the breeze,
I like to eat mice,
Better than twice,
I have lots of snowy, white feathers,
Which keep me warm,
In different weathers,
My favourite meal is a mouse,
I love to live in my treetop house,
I want to be free,
So don't capture me,
I love my family,
Who live in another tree,
I have a twin that helps me win,
I just so love to be me!

Nicholas Koczorowski (8)
St Edward's CE (VA) Primary School, Romford

Who Am I?

People buy me,
But never eat me,
They use forks and knives to take stuff out of me,
I am sad,
Taking my stuff,
Not even asking,
That's really tough,
No matter how large it is,
They never give up,
I have no eyes,
But I can sense some flies.

Angus Wong (9)
St Edward's CE (VA) Primary School, Romford

The Adventure And The Unknown Creature

As I stumbled, I couldn't believe what I saw.
Though deep down I was wishing for more, more, more.
Stepped on a branch. What had I done!
This was now the time, I must run, run, run!
I looked left, nothing.
I looked right, nothing.
Up and down, nothing.
Once I glanced back...
Run!
I must run otherwise my dreams are done.
Wolves chased me.
Why are they so fast?
I could hide!
Finally! At last!
Wolves were gone and my job was done!
Until... Woah!
Shh! What was that?
As soon as I saw this my heartbeat became slow at last!

I gazed in love at the beautiful, dazzling and shy unknown mystical creature.
Sharp eyes but precious.
My gorgeous dream had come true!
Should I show myself as a friendly sister
Or should I run as addressed to fate with the aggressive wolves?
I gathered confidence and rose up angelically.
Hush there.
Don't run.
Your beauty and humbleness attracted me to you.
You are special.
I'll name you Pegasus.

Annabel Odion-Amedu (10)
The Beacon CE Primary School, Liverpool

The Predator

Predators,
All part of the food chain,
Almost all violently vicious.
Attack and kill,
It's their only way!
But yet some lay on top of them all.
This one
Will reign supreme.
This one
Will be pristine.
With teeth as sharp as shards,
It bites for the final blow.
With a tail as strong as steel,
It takes all down low.
Scales as strong as silver,
No one can penetrate through.
Terror has struck with chaos in the form of doom.
With fire from its mouth,
It can alight the forest of its prey.
Killing the weak,

Harming the strong,
It strikes at night,
When it's gone dark.

Thejas Kashyap (11)
The Beacon CE Primary School, Liverpool

Just A Guardian Of A Mythical World?

While clouds drift in the sky like candyfloss,
Dragons among the fluffiness
Dart through, though invisible to mortals.
Though one I have glimpsed, one unforgettable, sticks like glue.
Serpent of the Seas and Skies.
Shiny scales glisten in the moonlight, silver
Sometimes known as the controller, guardian, emperor.
Sometimes known as the killer, monster.
Just a creature known to be mythical?
Or a dream, a possibility that transforms to reality?
Powerful, intelligent, strong,
Like a cloud,
Once it is reached, it is shattered,
I never saw the creature again...

Luo Xi Wu (10)
The Beacon CE Primary School, Liverpool

Surviving Summer

She saw the beautiful, glistening and calm ocean,
She was scared at first,
But then she felt an excited rush go through
her spine,
She dove in and saw a beautiful, shiny,
Calm and crazy fish with a stripy tail.
She swam out closer to the fish,
The fish took her to another part of the ocean,
She saw tons more beautiful fish,
Some shiny, some tiny,
Some with stripy tails and
Some with polka dot tails.
She tasted the salty water
And heard whales talking to other whales.
She knew this was where she belonged.

Sasha Thomas (9)
The Beacon CE Primary School, Liverpool

The Fabled Dragon

Liess on top of a mountain of gold.
Scales as strong as silver
And teeth as sharp as a diamond's point.
He has killed ten thousand men
And more are coming.
Eyes as red as blood
With skin as black as the night.
Enormous wings, bigger than a house.
A magnificent tail like never seen before.
Flies up to speeds faster than a fighter jet.
It feasts on only men.
Its fire is hotter than the inside of a volcano.
Beware of the beast, it might come for you too...

Corey Dunn (10)
The Beacon CE Primary School, Liverpool

Butterfly

As I fly across the River Thames,
Buckingham Palace and the beautiful plains,
I fly across the O2 Arena
And see the winter rain starting to get meaner,
Across the sky, I can see millions of people
And other tiny animals running around.
As I fly I can see the extravagant buildings that look as big as the universe
And see all of the bright yellow springs.

Today was a wonderful day and I can't wait for what tomorrow will bring!

Mosunmola Chrisitne Akinduro (11)
The Beacon CE Primary School, Liverpool

Tom's Journey

Tom loves the beeping cars,
But he loves exploring so he left sadly.
He sailed and zoomed in his wooden boat.

The river was waving like trees.
The hills were as big as mountains.
The spiky jungle hid the monkeys.

Tom and his boat travelled forever,
Even he didn't go far.
He went somewhere familiar,
But his adventure ended right where it started.
At home.

Michael Wong (6)
The Beacon CE Primary School, Liverpool

Tom's Journey

Tom loves cars zooming in the busy city,
But he wanted to explore some more.
He cruised away in his wooden boat.

The river was swaying next to the dazzling trees.
The hills rose over the sneaky foxes.
The green jungle hid the swaying vines.

Tom and his boat cruised far,
Even down a cold, scary waterfall,
But his adventure ended right where it started.
At home.

Georgia Ruddock (6)
The Beacon CE Primary School, Liverpool

Tom's Journey

Tom loved the humming cars in the city,
But he loved exploring so he left.
He cruised on his wooden boat.

The river splashed next to the green trees.
The hills towered over the cheeky fox.
The dark jungle hid the slithering snake.

Tom and his boat sailed and sailed,
Even past jungle and waterfalls,
But his adventure ended right where it started.
At home.

Chaitrika Yarramsetti (6)
The Beacon CE Primary School, Liverpool

Wild Animal

A soft, dark grey she-cat sat in the wind with a broad, flattened face.
Her eyes shimmered like gold.
Her fur ruffled like a dozen feathers.
Her claws unsheathed, she fell to the trees
And tumbled into a ditch.
The hole was empty, not a single heartbeat heard.
So she padded back to her soft, feathered bed,
Unaware of the dark shadow following her only one tail length away...

Eva-Jane Rylands (9)
The Beacon CE Primary School, Liverpool

Tom's Journey

Tom loved the park in the city,
But he wanted to explore new creatures.
He cruised away in a wooden boat.

The river rushed past the spooky trees.
The hills rose over the cheeky foxes.
The scary jungle hid the cheeky baboons.

Tom and his boat travelled far,
Even as far as jungles and waterfalls,
But his adventure ended right where it started.
At home.

Harry Kelly (6)
The Beacon CE Primary School, Liverpool

Below The Clouds

Down below me,
Soft, silky snowcats roaring through the dark, gloomy forest,
Free birds dancing on the gentle breeze,
Silent trees reaching towards the abyss away from gnawing insects from underneath me,
Spitting out snow, watching it descend,
The hidden hunters, unwavering patience, waiting for a moment of weakness,
An explosion of colours below, a tranquil world above.

Brân Parkinson (10)
The Beacon CE Primary School, Liverpool

Tom's Journey

Tom loved sailing and exploring,
But he wanted to see the water,
He zoomed away in his wooden boat.

The river was wavy and the trees were swaying.
The hills were wavy over and over.
The green jungle hid the treasure.

Tom and his boat travelled far away,
Even across an ocean you know,
But his adventure ended right where it started.
At home.

Jerryane Jaboro (6)
The Beacon CE Primary School, Liverpool

Over The Rainbow

R ed, the colour of love,
A lways see it high above,
I ndigo, purple, pink and more,
N ever stopping, never reaching the floor,
B lue, yellow, orange and green,
O ver the rainbow, like a movie scene.
W henever I invade the sky,
S top the rain, I want to say hi!

Mollie Finnigan (8)
The Beacon CE Primary School, Liverpool

A Pretty Fairy

I love to fly high,
I can do magic
And I can pick up flowers.
I am going to my friend's house.
I live in a castle
And I have pink wings.
I have a map
And I have a rainbow cup.
I have a little flower in my hair
And a dress with a belt.
I feel happy because I have a flower in my red hair.

Joanna Ko (5)
The Beacon CE Primary School, Liverpool

The Sea Lion

The sea lion sniffed the sea air.
It splashed at the sea which crept away
Slipping over the stones.
The next day I came and
His eyes were like giant stars.

The sea lion's family
Came to the shore
And I went and waved
On the beach.

They waved back
I saw them every day.

Florence Hunt (5)
The Beacon CE Primary School, Liverpool

Sticky Fingers

Hi, my name is Joseph
And stealing is my speciality.
If someone has riches,
Please don't be snitches so I can steal from them.
In the darkness or in the light, stealing is easier than easy.
Hiding in the shadows till member George comes out
With our master plans, we will be thieves around!

Jonathan Akhere (9)
The Beacon CE Primary School, Liverpool

Hendo The Hero

H ero of the match.
E verybody's captain.
N obody else compares.
D estined to be a leader.
E ntertaining millions of fans.
R unning across the pitch.
S coring lots of goals.
O pportunity opens up.
N o longer nil-nil, Hendo scores.

Billy-Ste Thompson (7)
The Beacon CE Primary School, Liverpool

Cat

The beautiful cat sits in the bright light until night
Suddenly another cat started a fight
The fight lasted till morning light appeared
The next day when the light disappeared
The cat had learned his lesson and decided to sleep tight until morning light appeared
Anxious and scared the night he feared.

Leela Talla (10)
The Beacon CE Primary School, Liverpool

Rosie's Journey

I can smell sweet, tasty flowers.
The flowers are far away
And I really want to see how they taste.
I will spread my glittery pink wings
And flutter to the tallest flower
In the enchanted dark field.
I wonder if I will see my friends there.
I feel very excited for my journey to the plants.

Rhiannon Parkinson (5)
The Beacon CE Primary School, Liverpool

Tree

I'm dark and green and very clean
You can bury me with a seed
Although I'm cut, I really thought one day I might learn to walk
Every day I see the birds that climb on top of me
The people below me rise and sing
The wind blows into me every day, making my leaves blow away.

Kiara-Rose Stevie Thompson (9)
The Beacon CE Primary School, Liverpool

What Am I?

I'm used every day from morning to evening.
I can come back to life with some electricity.
I get left in the boot of the car from nine o'clock.
I'm purple and I'm a Samsung.
No one likes me because of Apple.
What am I?

Answer: A phone.

Martha Tyrer (10)
The Beacon CE Primary School, Liverpool

The Joyful Fish

As the sea swayed happily, I was nearly eaten
By a big, bad beast as large as a door
Its teeth were sharp and its eyes were huge
Its mouth was about to open
On top of my little, feeble body
But I was pushed to safety towards the north of the sea
By my fierce friend.

Kimiko Yu (9)
The Beacon CE Primary School, Liverpool

Sitting In The Garden

As the trees sway in the breeze,
From my house I see the blue seas.
The birds soar over me,
As little girls scream.
After the little girls scream,
The sun roars back at them.
As the sunflowers sway in the breeze,
Some leaves fall off the bright green trees.

Onyinyechi Nkeze (9)
The Beacon CE Primary School, Liverpool

Enough

Sometimes I don't feel good enough
That is tough
My friends know more than me
It makes me feel dumb
Every night I cry to my mum
I told her, she said, "What are you good at?"
So I tried my best
Never give up because you're always enough.

Ese Azanuwha (11)
The Beacon CE Primary School, Liverpool

A Cat Called Kat

Hello human,
You can hear me?
Well, I am a cat called Kat (My name is cat just with a 'k')
No I don't wear a hat,
And I don't sit on a mat,
In fact I play dead on my human,
Sometimes I do hit my head,
But I usually land on my bed.

Chaaya Patel-Rourke (9)
The Beacon CE Primary School, Liverpool

Where Do Books Live?

I am a big house that should be quiet.
You can borrow and bring me back.
Small and big things are inside.
There are a lot of chairs inside.
Sometimes I have computers.
Every book is in me.
What am I?

Answer: A library.

Chloe Roberts (6)
The Beacon CE Primary School, Liverpool

Anfield Stadium

Anfield Stadium
Like a red beacon
Just a kick away
From Goodison
Red, blue, red, blue
The cheering gets louder.
The fans walk past
Cars beep and fireworks bang.
Football matches are exciting when you live
in Everton.

Kaedyn Phillips (5)
The Beacon CE Primary School, Liverpool

Harry Potter

H e is very magical but his broom is very 'fragical'.
A lthough he can fly he will always try.
R on is his friend and Hermione too.
R ival of Harry Potter is Malfoy.
Y ummy food at Hogwarts.

Mohammad Hassan (9)
The Beacon CE Primary School, Liverpool

Mr Jackson

T eacher at school.
E ncourages us to learn.
A lways being helpful.
C ares for us every day.
H elp us when we're stuck.
E ducating for the future.
R espects all children.

Stephen Chen (8)
The Beacon CE Primary School, Liverpool

My Dad

My dad plays Pokémon and Dragon Ball Z
Dad gives me Pokémon cards and games
My dad takes me to the park
And Daddy takes me to boxing.
Daddy took me to the zoo
And we saw the animals and then went home.

Alex Knowles (6)
The Beacon CE Primary School, Liverpool

The Titanic

The Titanic was gigantic
The Titanic was colossal
The Titanic was unsinkable
Until it hit an iceberg
Now the Titanic sleeps at the
Bottom of the ocean
Where its passengers are
Crabs and sharks.

Shay Smith (5)
The Beacon CE Primary School, Liverpool

YouTube

Y ou watch online
O ne million
U nder a secret name
T en million subscribers
U p go my posts
B eing popular
E veryone knows me
R eally good fun.

Himidi Majaliwa Mzungu (7)
The Beacon CE Primary School, Liverpool

Floating In Space Lost

S eeing all the planets and the stars.
P lanes down below.
A little piece of glowstone pinched me.
C an I ever go back down onto Earth?
E ntering the blackness up above.

Max Sudbury (7)
The Beacon CE Primary School, Liverpool

Learning Together

S upporting our friends
C hoosing our future
H oping to be the best
O pportunities to succeed
O ur school in the lead
L earning together, following Jesus.

Rock Liu (7)
The Beacon CE Primary School, Liverpool

Always In My Heart

Roses are red, violets are blue,
Even though I can't see you,
I still miss you.
Even when we're miles apart,
I always have you in my heart.
My memories mean we will never be apart.

Ivy Jones (8)
The Beacon CE Primary School, Liverpool

Meerkat

M y fur is brown
E scape my burrow
E nter the wary
R eally weird noises
K eep finding food
A ll around I explore
T hen time to go to sleep.

Poppy Kegan (7)
The Beacon CE Primary School, Liverpool

Pharaoh

P yramids are where I'm buried
H e is in charge
A king
R ich ruler
A ncient Egyptian
O nly one can rule
H ieroglyphics write my name.

Ivy Robinson (7)
The Beacon CE Primary School, Liverpool

Unicorn

U nder the stars I jump,
N ever stop believing
I n magic,
C andy canes grow in my hair,
O ver the
R ainbow
N ow adventures await.

Florence Royal (7)
The Beacon CE Primary School, Liverpool

Super Space

S tars shining everywhere
P lanets orbiting the sun
A stronauts roaming on the moon
C omets trying to hit everyone
E arth is our only home.

Lucas Wang (7)
The Beacon CE Primary School, Liverpool

The Princess

The princess has the most finest dresses
And glittering crown
A fabulous tie
Beautiful shoes
The finest graces
She was the most beautiful ever seen.

Natalia Oraseanu (5)
The Beacon CE Primary School, Liverpool

My Puppy

M ellow dog
Y ellow dog

P erfect
U nited with me
P uptaculous
P ineapple perfect
Y ay dog.

Nancy Knowles (8)

The Beacon CE Primary School, Liverpool

The Greatest Ever

M esmerisingly quick
E xtremely talented
S o many Ballon d'Ors
S urprisingly super
I ncredible goals.

Darren Odion-Amedu (8)
The Beacon CE Primary School, Liverpool

The Best

M ake me happy
Y ummy food

M e and my mum love maths
U nique
M agnificent mum.

Darcey McGuinness (8)
The Beacon CE Primary School, Liverpool

Lion

L oud in the jungle
I hunt prey
O nwards I run
N ever defeated.

Khalaf Husain (8)

The Beacon CE Primary School, Liverpool

An Astronaut In Space

I see the beautiful twinkling stars,
I watch a camera head toward Mars,
I float like a cloud when we arrive on the moon,
Our jumps are huge when we arrive on the moon,
Space rocks fly about as I float about,
Earth glistens from a distance,
I see brilliant views in space,
We put on helmets before we're out of the rocket,
I put my helmet shades down so I don't see the sun,
Shadows of shapes sit in the distance like planets,
Then we send pictures to Earth,
And check the wires are intact,
We steer the ship,
We protect our equipment,
Being an astronaut is fun but also hard.

Amelia Muzammil (10)
The Godolphin Junior Academy, Slough

A Point Of View From An Owl

Tu-whit, tu-whoo it was time to seek food for food,
As I flew above the water, which was a bath of soapy water,
Now, what to eat?
Some crunchy, juicy worms?
Oh, or a slow snail?
As I flew through the green, swaying trees
That was calling someone to come pluck
Its big, juicy oranges.
I swayed down to eat a fat, juicy worm,
My feathers touched the green, dark grass
Which felt like sitting on a thousand cushions.
I took a fat pink worm and then...
Gulp! It was gone.
Then I saw dread.
The horrible, blinding dawn was coming!
I jumped into flying mode and flew.
Faster and faster,
My wings were on the brink of death,
Like a man almost falling off a cliff.

I finally was at home.
Phew, I was not going back,
To that derelict forest any time soon.

Mohammed Rayyan Hussain (9)
The Godolphin Junior Academy, Slough

I Wish I Was A Supergirl!

If I was a supergirl,
I would wish I could fly,
And race birds in the sky.
If I was a supergirl,
I would have all the powers,
For jumping over tall towers.
If I was a supergirl,
I would save all the poor,
Make them rich and hungry no more.
If I was a supergirl,
I would save all the oceans,
And stop the pollution.
If I was a supergirl,
The world would change.
All because of me!

Aliza Latif (9)
The Godolphin Junior Academy, Slough

YouTuber Boy

I'm a YouTuber boy
I'm a YouTuber boy
I like to play games all day long
I'm an awesome YouTuber
I'm a terrific gamer
I can't stop playing video games
I want to get two million subscribers
I never get a headache out of games
I want to make my own video game
So kids can play my video game
I'm a YouTuber boy
I'm a YouTuber boy.

Zakariyya Azam (7)
The Godolphin Junior Academy, Slough

Hat-Trick Hero

Game starts.
Nerve-racking.
Leicester scored! Oh no!
Penalty retaken. One-nil.
Now I am frustrated.
So close.
Harry Kane header.
Now it's one-all.
Now we're back in the game.
Corner.
My heart is beating as fast as a cheetah.
Dier! Yes! Goal!
The crowd is as loud as an elephant.
No! Maddison scores again against Tottenham.
Two-all.
Bentancur is through with the ball in his feet.
Bentancur!
His first goal for Tottenham. Half-time. Three-two.
Second half.
I'm very nervous.
Sixtieth minute.

A legend.
Sonny comes on.
Oh, Sonny, he's so close.
Yes, it's in the net. What a goal!
Right in the top bins.
It's Sonny again. From the same position as before.
Yes! Sonny scores again.
Sonny's like a fish in the ocean.
He's running fast.
Yes! It's through!
Hat-trick for Sonny.
Oh no! Possible off-side.
Yes! On side!
My hat-trick hero.
Six-two in the end.

Teddy Shaw (8)
Thomas's Academy, Fulham

Minnie's Life

M innie was our first pet
I loved cuddling and playing with her
N ot that she was always that happy
N osing around, looking for places to hide and climb
I magining a life out of her cage
E scaping, never far from her mind, and she was often successful!
S he was so kind and playful!

L ife for her was an adventure, full of mysteries
I mpatiently waiting for us to feed her
F illing her cheeks with monkeys nuts and sunflower seeds
E njoying her life in our family. We'll miss you, Minnie!

Mia Sweeting (10)
Thomas's Academy, Fulham

The Football Game

Football is a very nice sport.
When I run on the pitch, I feel the fresh air in
my lungs.
I am thinking about the best day ever.
It is a very nice day.
I can touch a very strongly shot ball in my hands.
I feel the spiky grass on my feet.

I feel fantastic!
I feel my muscles grow as I run.
My dribbling accuracy is very good.
It is eighty-nine rating,
But when I lose the ball,
Someone slide-tackles me
And I take a fall.

I take the ball and I just feel too nervous,
And a goal!
One-nil to our team.
I am happy.

Christopher Stankov (9)
Thomas's Academy, Fulham

Flowers, Flowers, Everywhere

It was winter
The flowers were closed
No flowers were singing
All cosy while it snowed

It changed to spring
The flowers bloomed and sang
They cheered people up
Each and every one!

Next came summer
They still sang their song
But some were dying, sadly
Among the splashes and the splongs

Finally came autumn.
The flowers, their eyes hard as rocks!
I felt so sad, I could barely do a splosh.

Francisco Barreto (8)
Thomas's Academy, Fulham

A Life Of A Baby

The baby is cranky like a rain cloud,
Wa, wa, waaa,
The egg head baby maybe needs milk,
Small like a doll, the adorable baby might be hungry,
Wa, wa, waaa,
No milk,
Nappies, wipes, maybe he needs changing,
Soft as a pillow the baby rolled over,
Wa, wa, waaa,
No changing,
Swaddle, maybe he's tired,
Snug like a pig in a blanket,
Finally, the baby is asleep.

Bella Shaw (10)
Thomas's Academy, Fulham

The Life Of Maui The Cat

M any people think I'm as silly as a sheep and as funny as a frog.
A t home, my life is calm, cosy, quiet and peaceful and all I do is eat, sleep, drink, watch birds and play.
U sually, when I'm on holiday I have lots of fun.
I climb as high as the clouds and like to run around, exploring new places and finding interesting creatures that are new to me.

Olivia Hart (9)
Thomas's Academy, Fulham

The Peaceful Waves

One summer's day I went to the ocean.
I soaked my feet in the icy water
Where I saw the most beautiful view.
I saw small, calm and graceful waves.
They were every shade of blue.
The waves rippled in the sunlight.
The sun was so bright it reflected on
The water like glitter.
At the end of the day,
The soft waves shrank
As they drifted away.

Zaina Marafi (8)
Thomas's Academy, Fulham

Jephrey The Second

Fast and slick like a dart through the water,
Stealthy as a submarine but still can be heard,
Searching his tank like a curious explorer,
The sun shines through making his reflection blurred,

Underwater mysteries to unravel,
To be one of them would be my wish,
Making bubbling noises and spitting gravel,
What a life it would be, to be my fish.

Rafe Watkins (9)
Thomas's Academy, Fulham

Dogs

D ogs are fun, dogs are great, dogs can run and jump and play,
O h how I wish I had a dog, they're so cute and playful and loving,
G o and get one for me Mum, go and get one for me Dad,
S ome are grey and some are brown, some are white and some are black, there are lots of different types of dogs like spaniels, like shepherds, like terriers!

Ayana Al Iskandar-Sabrosa (9)
Thomas's Academy, Fulham

The Sun Speaks About Climate Change

I rose over the sky
Over the atmosphere
And among the stars
I saw the Earth
So far away and tiny to me

When I looked close
I saw so much rain
And clouds heavy like an anvil
And thick like a swamp
I saw the Earth
Choking, crying, dying

I set and I was sad
Heavy with fear

What will happen to me?

Xavier Elliott-Richards (8)
Thomas's Academy, Fulham

Imagine If...

Imagine if you could live off your passion.
Imagine if your weekly wage was in the millions.
Imagine if people would cheer your name when they saw you.
But, imagine if you were stopped on the road when people recognised you.
Imagine if people only saw the bad side of you.
Imagine if you were a famous football player.

Emile Toromanoff (9)
Thomas's Academy, Fulham

Dragon

D ark in a cave, dragons live,
R ight when the sunset falls, dragons come out,
A t a second they will eat you up,
G ot a bag of water bottles for a dragon's tummy is hot,
O n a dragon feels like a roller coaster
N ear the end of the dragon, spikes everywhere.

Neel Patel (9)
Thomas's Academy, Fulham

Sunny Weather

I like the sunny weather
It feels warm on my face
It makes me feel happy

I like the sunny weather
It shines so bright in the sky
It makes me feel happy

I like the sunny weather
It gives life to the plants
It makes me feel happy.

Santino Ferrari (8)
Thomas's Academy, Fulham

Typical Trees

T he nature surrounds the tree
R aking leaves
E arth hanging below the tree, feeding it nutrients
to help it bloom
E nchanted trees are everywhere, hard to find,
but not unfeasible.

Antonio Ferrari (10)
Thomas's Academy, Fulham

Happiness

A lot of things make me happy
When I don't have my favourite food
It makes me unhappy
I enjoy playing games
I enjoy being on a plane
I enjoy playing with my friends till the day ends.

Kobe James
Thomas's Academy, Fulham

What Am I?

A kennings poem

Track follower
Speedy carrier
Metal runner
Underground adventurer
Commuter partner
What am I?

Answer: I am an efficient Tube train.

Owen Chi Hang Choi (9)

Thomas's Academy, Fulham

A Coal Miner's Needs, Loves And Life

Pitch-black,
Noises in the eerie dark,
Clanging, hacking, chippings,
Miners mining, spades digging,
Men climbing down ladders,
Down in the dirty dark,
Spiders lurk, don't make a spark!
Otherwise you might,
Explode some dynamite,
Or some lethal gas.
You'll smell coal and sweat,
Feeling rock coal and pick-axes
After a day's work, your hands are full of blisters,
Nothing but coal, ladders, dirt, sweat and dark,
Stay thin so you don't get stuck!
Love the dark, love the mining,
See, do and love all this,
My darling, oh bliss,
You're a coal miner!

Finlay Ferguson
Whitley Chapel CE First School, Steel

Coal Miner

Dark hole,
Soot and coal up your nose,
All the horrible smells,
Driest of throats,
Hungry and thirsty,
No water to be seen,
No faces to be seen,
Just black and white,
No money for you,
Mining all day, tiring day,
Black face, black hands,
Dark hole,
Nothing to see but black and white,
Going home,
Into your bed, goodnight,
Black of night,
Sleeping in the night,
What will you eat?
Not a thing just black and white,
Nothing to smell but the scent of the mines,

At home black of night,
In your bed, goodnight.

Hazel Lea
Whitley Chapel CE First School, Steel

A Day Of Sewing

People, gloves, and thread are what I see,
I smell urine faintly, chemicals and leather too,
My ears hear sighs and snips and rustles,
The feel of the needle going through the leather,
In... out, in... out. To make people leather gloves.
It is strenuous work, pulling the needle through the leather!
My arms shall start to ache soon!
At the end of the day, I feel satisfied, tired, weak,
And cold, but proud of the gloves I made.
My day of strenuous sewing is over!

Claudia Deasy (8)
Whitley Chapel CE First School, Steel

Tanning

Whiffy wee,
Smelly stripping,
Long leather,
Satisfying sewing.
Chemicals rippling and burbling in their tub.
Needles to thread to
Animal skins,
Chemicals streaming
Into dirty rivers.
Who knows what could be in them?
Hard-working people pushing
Hides down in wee.
Being loaded onto pack ponies and being
Carted away to market.
Being bought by people from all over the world.
To be made into gorgeous gloves, bags and hats.

Libby Reed (7)

Whitley Chapel CE First School, Steel

The Scary Mines

Off we go to the mines
Chipping again
Guys!
Come on
We need to get
Thundering amounts
Of that stinky coal
And get
Jet-black skin
Lamps hanging off the miners' belts
Minecarts rattling
Rattle, rattle, rattle, rattle
Chug, chug, chug
Bang, bang, bang!
Off we go
Off we go to the conveyor belts
Up, up, up, up, up it goes to the top.

Freddie Stephenson (8)
Whitley Chapel CE First School, Steel

Sewers Working

Pin a needle through the leather.
Sewer sewing, *sew, sew, sew.*
Push the needle out and in.
Sewer sewing, *sew, sew, sew.*
Carrying on pushing it.
Sewer sewing, *sew, sew, sew.*
Arms exhausted, not giving up.
Sewer sewing, *sew, sew, sew.*
Sewing gloves for winter's cold.
Sewer sewing, *sew, sew, sew.*

Owen Francksen
Whitley Chapel CE First School, Steel

YOUNG WRITERS INFORMATION

We hope you have enjoyed reading this book – and that you will continue to in the coming years.

If you're the parent or family member of an enthusiastic poet or story writer, do visit our website **www.youngwriters.co.uk/subscribe** and sign up to receive news, competitions, writing challenges and tips, activities and much, much more! There's lots to keep budding writers motivated!

If you would like to order further copies of this book, or any of our other titles, then please give us a call or order via your online account.

Young Writers
Remus House
Coltsfoot Drive
Peterborough
PE2 9BF
(01733) 890066
info@youngwriters.co.uk

Join in the conversation!
Tips, news, giveaways and much more!